Vinny and Chip

Written by Tomi Saga
Illustrated by Mackenzie Ott

Vinny the cat lived in a small country town. One day, he was thirsty, so he went to the river's edge to drink some fresh water.

As he was drinking, he noticed a little field mouse swimming by, paddling his little legs quickly and squeaking, "Help me! help me! There's an alligator coming down the river after me!"

Vinny said, "I'll help you. Just jump on my back."

So, the mouse crawled up Vinny's front leg, got on his back, and held on.

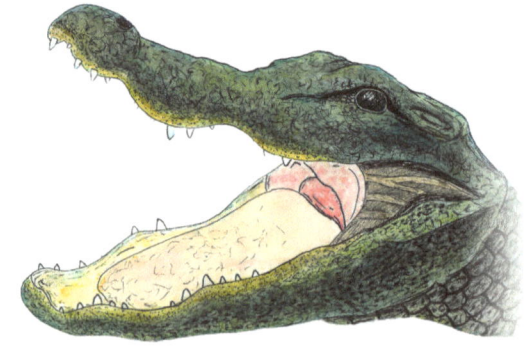

But before Vinny could ask the mouse his name, the alligator popped his head out of the river with his mouth wide open, revealing all his sharp teeth!

All at once, Vinny bravely hunched his back, hissed loudly, and showed his sharp teeth too.

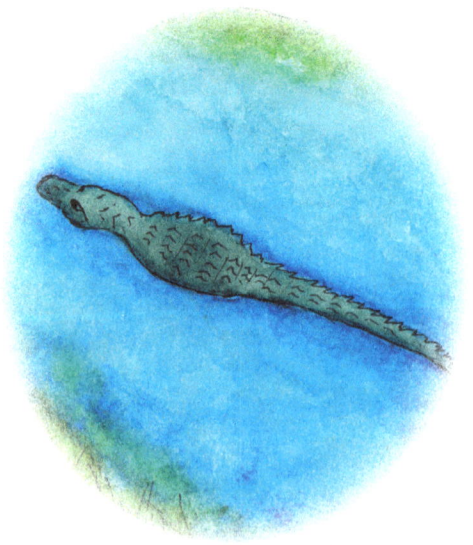

The alligator, seeing a much smaller animal who was not scared of him, decided not to bother with a cat and continued cruising down the river.

Vinny left the edge of the river with the mouse still hanging on his back, and they began to talk. "My name is Chip. Do you plan on eating me?" the mouse asked.

"I do not plan on eating you, little mouse. You are my friend now. I will take you to your home." So, Vinny walked a while until they saw an old barn house.

Chip climbed down, said thanks, and scurried down a little hole on the side of the barn. When Chip got inside his mouse house, he told all his family members, all fifty of them, that if they are ever faced with danger from a big animal, all they have to do is hunch their backs, show their teeth, and hiss loudly. He showed his family exactly what Vinny did when they saw the alligator that day.

The next day, Chip and his mouse family were outside in the field near the barn, looking for acorns and seeds to eat, when along came a snake, moving slowly in the tall grass.

"A snake! A snake! Danger!" Chip shouted to all the mice, all fifty of them. "Remember what to do! Show your teeth, hunch your back, and hiss loudly like a cat!"

And they all did, all together, just that. When the snake saw all their teeth and heard all the loud hissing, he decided not to bother with them and slithered on past them, leaving them behind.

Time went by, and one day the mice were eating seeds and acorns in the field when they heard a cat meowing. They looked up, and it was Vinny, up in a tree. "What's wrong? Why don't you come down?" said Chip to the cat.

"There's a fox that's trying to eat me," Vinny said.

No sooner did he say that when a big fox appeared under the tree with his front paws on the trunk and his sharp teeth showing.

"Let's show him, boys," said Chip, calling all the mice. But this time, they did something different. They stacked themselves onto each other's shoulders until they made a pyramid shape, and it made them look really big! All fifty of them—well, all ninety of them. (Their family was growing.)

The fox looked at the big pyramid of mice before him, all hissing, waving their arms and tails, showing their teeth, and he got confused. He growled at them and thought to himself, *This is very weird. I'm out of here*, and he turned and walked away.

When the fox was gone, Vinny climbed down the tree and looked at all the mice. He walked over to them and said, "You did a great job at scaring that fox."

Chip answered, "That's what friends do. We learned it from you!"

Chip and his brave mouse family went back to their mouse house, and Vinny remained longtime friends with all of his mouse buddies.

For my mother Eva who read us wonderful children's books and all my beautiful and crazy grandchildren: Shareef, Adale, Ashraf, Aubree, Belen, Eva, Noah, Matias, Layla, Joseph, Elias and Flora – with love. –TS

Copyright © 2021 by Tomi Saga

Published by Tomi Elsagga. For permission requests or ordering information, please contact: catintheattic789@gmail.com

Illustrations by Mackenzie Ott.

All rights reserved. No part of this publication may be reproduced, distributed, or transmitted in any form or by any means, including photocopying, recording, or other electronic or mechanical methods without prior written permission from the publisher, except in the case of brief quotations embodied in critical reviews and certain other noncommercial uses permitted by copyright law.

ISBN 978-1-7375548-0-6 (hardcover) • ISBN 978-1-7375548-1-3 (paperback)
ISBN 978 -1-7375548-2-0 (ebook)

Book design by the Virtual Paintbrush. Text was set in Goudy Oldstyle.